THE
NBA
A HISTORY OF HOOPS

Published by Creative Education
P.O. Box 227, Mankato, Minnesota 56002
Creative Education is an imprint of The Creative Company
www.thecreativecompany.us

Design and production by Christine Vanderbeek
Art direction by Rita Marshall

Printed by Corporate Graphics in the United States of America

Photographs by Alamy (Travelshots), Dreamstime (Munktcu), Getty Images
(Issac Baldizon/NBAE, Victor Baldizon/NBAE, Andrew D. Bernstein/NBAE,
Nathaniel S. Butler/NBAE, Lou Capozzola/NBAE, Jesse D. Garrabrant/NBAE,
Barry Gossage/NBAE, Frazer Harrison, Andy Lyons/Allsport, Fernando Medina/
NBAE, Layne Murdoch/NBAE, Greg Nelson/Sports Illustrated, Bob Rosato/
Sports Illustrated, SM/AIUEO, Alexander Tamargo), iStockphoto (Brandon
Laufenberg), US Presswire (Mark J. Rebilas)

Library of Congress Cataloging-in-Publication Data
Hetrick, Hans.
The story of the Miami Heat / by Hans Hetrick.
p. cm. — (The NBA: a history of hoops)
Includes index.
Summary: The history of the Miami Heat professional basketball
team from its start in 1988 to today, spotlighting the franchise's
greatest players and reliving its most dramatic moments.
ISBN 978-1-58341-950-2
1. Miami Heat (Basketball team)—History—Juvenile literature. I. Title.
GV885.52.M53H48 2010   796.323'6409759381—dc22   2009035027

CPSIA: 120109 PO1093

First Edition
2 4 6 8 9 7 5 3 1

Page 3: Forward Michael Beasley
Pages 4–5: Heat fans during the 2006 NBA Finals

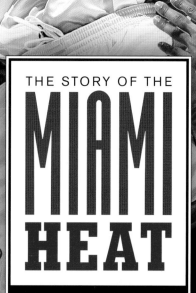

THE STORY OF THE

MIAMI
HEAT

HANS HETRICK

CREATIVE EDUCATION

CONTENTS

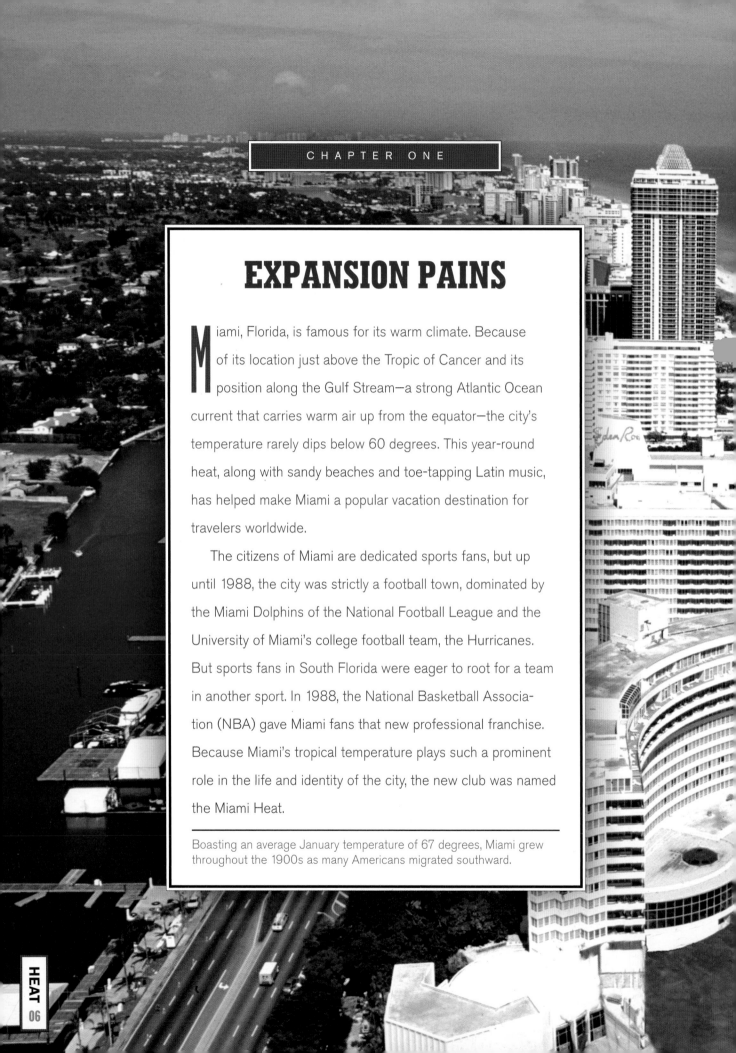

CHAPTER ONE

EXPANSION PAINS

Miami, Florida, is famous for its warm climate. Because of its location just above the Tropic of Cancer and its position along the Gulf Stream—a strong Atlantic Ocean current that carries warm air up from the equator—the city's temperature rarely dips below 60 degrees. This year-round heat, along with sandy beaches and toe-tapping Latin music, has helped make Miami a popular vacation destination for travelers worldwide.

The citizens of Miami are dedicated sports fans, but up until 1988, the city was strictly a football town, dominated by the Miami Dolphins of the National Football League and the University of Miami's college football team, the Hurricanes. But sports fans in South Florida were eager to root for a team in another sport. In 1988, the National Basketball Association (NBA) gave Miami fans that new professional franchise. Because Miami's tropical temperature plays such a prominent role in the life and identity of the city, the new club was named the Miami Heat.

Boasting an average January temperature of 67 degrees, Miami grew throughout the 1900s as many Americans migrated southward.

IN THE MID-1980S, WHEN THE NBA DECIDED TO EXPAND FROM 23 TEAMS TO 27, MIAMI WAS AN IDEAL CANDIDATE TO RECEIVE AN NBA FRANCHISE. The city was growing rapidly and in the midst of a cultural renaissance, as hundreds of local organizations in the arts and sciences were being founded and flourishing. With only the National Football League's Miami Dolphins in town, there was plenty of room for another professional sports team. So the Miami Sports and Exhibition Authority endorsed an investment group led by NBA Hall of Fame player Billy Cunningham, former sports agent Lewis Schaffel, and former Broadway producer Zev Buffman to begin wooing the NBA expansion committee. Between the allure of Miami and the formidable investment group, the city had a strong case. But it wasn't until Carnival Cruise Lines founder Ted Arison, who would become the club's majority owner, came on board with financial backing that the Miami group's proposal became irresistible. "Something big was happening in Miami," NBA commissioner David Stern remembered. "Something big in terms of the revitalization of the city. And we wanted to be part of that growth."

COURTSIDE STORIES

BECOMING THE HEAT

Burnie, the Miami Heat mascot.

At the time the Heat were born, the NBA was thriving, thanks largely to the appeal of superstars such as Boston Celtics forward Larry Bird, Los Angeles Lakers guard Magic Johnson, and Chicago Bulls guard Michael Jordan. To take advantage of this boom in popularity, the NBA had decided to expand from 23 teams to 27. The expansion would occur in two phases: the Charlotte Hornets and Miami Heat would be admitted in the 1988–89 season, and the Minnesota Timberwolves and Orlando Magic in 1989–90.

The original Miami starting lineup featured three veterans, point guard Rory Sparrow and forwards Billy Thompson and Pat Cummings, and two rookies, center Rony Seikaly and guard Kevin Edwards. On November 5, 1988, before a sold-out crowd in Miami Arena, head coach Ron Rothstein's Heat squad took the floor against the Los Angeles Clippers for its inaugural NBA game, losing 111–91. It was the start of what would be a painful season, even by first-year expansion team standards. The young Heat set an NBA record by losing their first 17 games. On December 14, the team finally pulled out an 89–88 road win against the Clippers for its first victory. Miami went on to finish with a league-worst 15–67 record.

The Heat had a fruitful 1989 NBA Draft, nabbing sharpshooting forward Glen Rice from the University of Michigan in the first round and crafty point guard Sherman Douglas from Syracuse University in the second. Although Rice and Douglas would have their share of productive seasons in Heat uniforms, Miami continued to struggle in 1989–90. The team improved its record by only three wins, going 18–64. Seikaly provided most of the season's highlights, averaging 16.6 points and 10.4 rebounds a game.

With the promising young trio of Douglas, Rice, and Seikaly, the Heat could attack opposing defenses in three ways. Douglas could penetrate from the point position and slash to the basket. Rice established his outside jump shot as one of the most lethal in the game. And Seikaly provided muscle and combativeness down low. Miami improved to 24–58 in the 1990–91 campaign but remained in the Eastern Conference's Atlantic Division cellar. "The Heat have put together a nice group of kids," said Pat Riley, then the coach of the Los Angeles Lakers. "If they give them some time to grow up, they'll have a good team."

COURTSIDE STORIES

THE EXPANSION CHAMPIONS

Rory Sparrow in action in 1989.

BECAUSE THE MIAMI HEAT AND THE CHARLOTTE HORNETS BOTH ENTERED THE NBA AS EXPANSION TEAMS IN 1988, A RIVALRY BLOSSOMED BETWEEN THE TWO. The franchises built their rosters in contrasting fashion. The Hornets signed mostly veteran players in an effort to win quickly, while the Heat aimed to develop young players for the long haul. On February 17, 1989, the Hornets and Heat met for the first time in what would turn out to be a nail-biting expansion team showdown. Late in the game, which was played in Miami, Heat guard Rory Sparrow blocked a shot by Hornets guard Muggsy Bogues, who had broken into the open court for what seemed an easy layup. Sparrow also came up with a big three-point shot to tie the game at 100, then he put the Hornets away with a buzzer-beating turnaround shot from the free-throw line, sending the Miami crowd into a frenzy. Ira Winderman, a *Miami Sun-Sentinel* sportswriter, put the win in perspective, noting, "The Charlotte game was that first really emotional game for the fans where they had something special to celebrate."

BEFORE THEIR INAUGURAL SEASON, THE HEAT SELECTED RONY SEIKALY AS THE NINTH OVERALL PICK IN THE 1988 NBA DRAFT. "I had a lot of high expectations for myself to put this franchise on my back," he said, "and I worked as hard as I could to help this franchise." Seikaly put in such effort, in fact, that he was named the NBA's Most Improved Player after the 1989–90 season. Nicknamed "The Spin Doctor" due to his trademark spin moves in the post, Seikaly was integral in establishing a foundation for the fledgling franchise. By the time the center was traded away in 1994, Miami had made two playoff appearances and improved its record to 42–40. During his tenure with the Heat, Seikaly averaged double digits in both points and rebounds per game and developed a reputation as a ferocious competitor. Heat guard Rory Sparrow explained, "He didn't care what happened to him physically when he was in the battle." After retiring in 1999, Seikaly returned to Miami, bought season tickets, and became one of the Heat's biggest fans.

CHAPTER TWO

THE HEAT START RISING

In the 1991 NBA Draft, the Heat selected Steve Smith, a versatile guard from Michigan State University. A superb ball handler, Smith could play point guard, yet at 6-foot-7, he could also be a force under the basket. Smith filled the chinks in the Heat's armor, helping new coach Kevin Loughery lead Miami to a 38–44 record and the eighth seed in the 1992 Eastern Conference playoffs. Even though they were quickly dispatched by Michael Jordan and the Bulls, the Heat earned the distinction of becoming the first of the four expansion teams of the late '80s to appear in the postseason.

Early in the 1992–93 season, Smith went down with a knee injury, and Miami fell into a 13–27 hole. The young guard returned to the lineup at midseason, but the team finished the year just 36–46 and came up short of a return trip to the play-offs. Before the start of the next season, Rice challenged his teammates. "We're not kids anymore," he said. "The fans have been patient with us. Now it's time to reward them."

Steve Smith (bottom) improved year by year, raising his scoring average in 4 Heat seasons to a high of 20.5 points a game by 1994–95.

The 1993–94 Heat answered their sharpshooter's call and finished 42–40, the franchise's first winning mark. Rice led the charge with 21.1 points per game. Entering the playoffs as the eighth seed, Miami faced the top-seeded Atlanta Hawks. In Game 1, the Heat came from behind in the fourth quarter to secure the franchise's first playoff win. Rice, Seikaly, and company pushed the heavily favored Hawks to a decisive Game 5 before losing the series.

Despite the club's progress—having just run neck-and-neck with an Eastern Conference heavyweight in the playoffs—the Heat underwent a major overhaul in the 1994 off-season. Seikaly was traded to the Golden State Warriors for athletic forward Billy Owens, and Smith and forward Grant Long were sent to Atlanta in exchange for muscular center Kevin Willis. Coach Loughery moved to a position in the team's front office, and Alvin Gentry took his place as head coach.

Willis, a long-armed seven-footer, had consistently put up big numbers in Atlanta, and early on, Willis and Rice were one of the league's highest-scoring duos. Rice cemented his status as one of the league's best shooters, finishing 9th in the NBA in scoring (22.3 points per game) as he rained down scores of three-point bombs. Ultimately,

though, the roster shakeup backfired. Willis was plagued by injury in the second half of the season, and the Heat ended the year a disappointing 32–50.

After that setback season, the Heat really shook things up. On September 2, 1995, Miami hired Pat Riley as the franchise's new president and head coach. Riley arrived with a most impressive resumé. As coach of the Lakers and the New York Knicks, Riley had won 4 NBA championships, taken his teams to the playoffs every year (13 straight), and won 50 or more games in each season as a head coach. "We're going to build this franchise into a winner the only way I know how," Riley told reporters when he arrived in Miami. "We're going to bring in the best players, and we'll work harder than anyone else."

Riley didn't waste any time bringing in the players he wanted. The

first item on the coach's wish list was a franchise center. In Los Angeles

and New York, Riley had built his teams around dominant centers

Kareem Abdul-Jabbar and Patrick Ewing respectively. On the eve of

the regular season, Riley landed one of the NBA's best big men when

the Heat traded Rice, center Matt Geiger, and guard Khalid Reeves to

the Hornets for All-Star center Alonzo Mourning. Guard Pete Myers and

forward LeRon Ellis also came to Miami as part of the swap.

ut Riley wasn't done. Midway through the 1995–96 season, he sent

Willis and guard Bimbo Coles to the Warriors for forward Chris Gatling

and lightning-quick point guard Tim Hardaway. After Riley's historic

flurry of trades, the Heat were virtually unrecognizable; only one player

from the previous year, forward Keith Askins, remained on the roster.

INTRODUCING...
GLEN RICE

POSITION FORWARD
HEIGHT 6-FOOT-7
HEAT SEASONS 1989–95

AS A BOY IN FLINT, MICHIGAN, GLEN RICE SPENT MUCH OF HIS CHILDHOOD AT THE PLAYGROUND WITH HIS BROTHER, SHOOTING BASKETS WELL INTO THE NIGHT. After that, Rice always believed, "If I can shoot the ball at night, it shouldn't be any problem when the lights come on." During his 15 years in the NBA, the lights were on as Rice dropped in 18,336 points' worth of shots. Rice was a sharpshooter extraordinaire, but if a defender tried to play him tight, he could also blow past him with his explosive first step. Rice led the University of Michigan to a 1989 college championship with a tournament-record 184 total points before he was drafted by the Heat in 1989 as the fourth overall pick. The rangy forward was the pure scorer Miami had lacked. In 1991–92, he led the team in scoring, helping Miami make its very first playoff appearance. In his five seasons with the Heat, Rice set many club records, including a 56-point effort versus the Orlando Magic in 1995 that, 15 years later, still stood as the highest one-game total by any Miami player.

CHAPTER THREE

A RIVALRY BOILS

The new-look Heat finished 42–40 in 1995–96 and kept Riley's streak of playoff appearances alive. In the postseason, they were swept in the first round by the 72–10 Bulls (who were on their way to claiming their fourth NBA crown in six seasons), but Miami fans were confident that their team was on the upswing.

The Heat did indeed surge to new heights, capturing their first Atlantic Division title in 1996–97 with a 61–21 record. Two new additions, sturdy swingman Dan Majerle and big-bodied forward P. J. Brown, helped the Heat suffocate opponents on defense, while Hardaway and Mourning carried most of the scoring load. The Heat relied on their home-court advantage to win a five-game series versus the Magic in the opening round of the 1997 playoffs. In round two, the Heat met Riley's old team, the Knicks. Heat broadcaster Jim

Although nicknamed "Thunder Dan" due to the power of his dunks, Dan Majerle was actually better known for his three-point shooting.

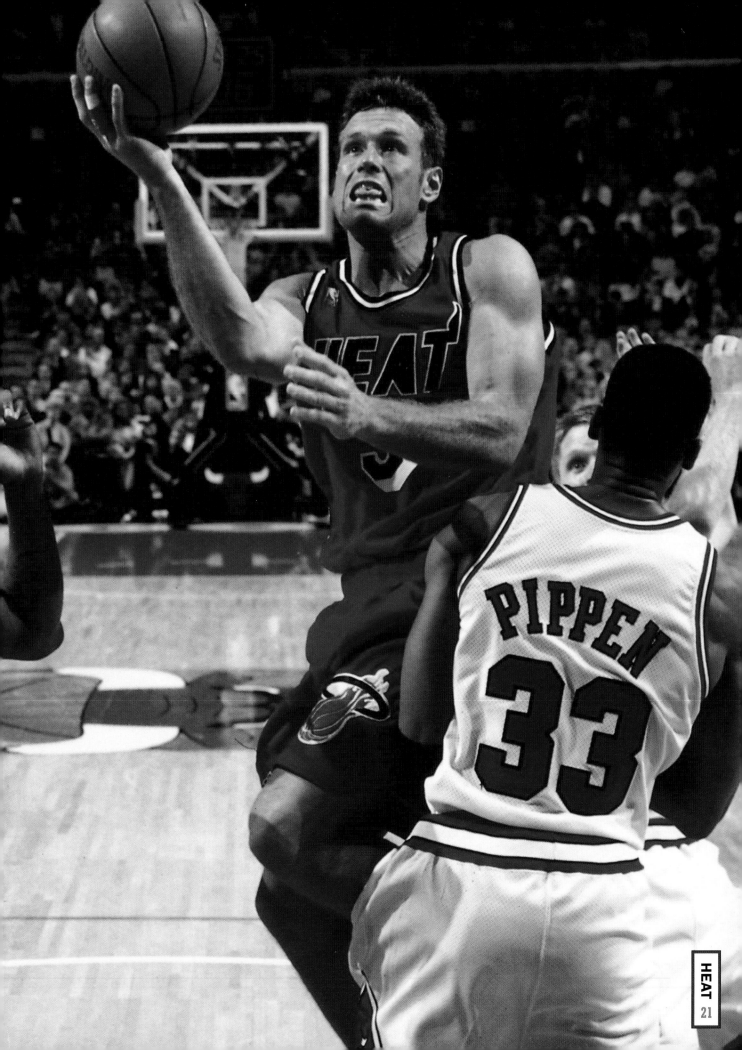

Berry saw a fierce battle coming. "This was going to be a rivalry on so many levels," he later said. "It was Pat Riley against his old team. It was Alonzo Mourning versus Patrick Ewing."

The Knicks took control early, jumping out to a three-games-to-one lead in the best-of-seven series, but momentum turned in the Heat's favor in Game 5 when, during a tussle under the basket, Brown flipped Knicks guard Charlie Ward over his hip and into the crowd, and a melee ensued. When the skirmish ended, the Knicks had lost Ewing, Ward, and guard Allan Houston to suspensions for Game 6 and forward Larry Johnson and guard John Starks for Game 7, while the Heat lost Brown for both games. The Heat won Game 5, and then—with the Knicks' best players in street clothes—Miami won the last two games and the series. The Heat advanced to their first Eastern Conference finals, only to fall to the Bulls in five games.

COURTSIDE STORIES

SHORT-HANDED BUT ON TARGET

Rex Chapman fires from long-range over Bulls star Michael Jordan.

IN FEBRUARY 1996, COACH PAT RILEY AND THE HEAT PUT TO-GETHER A BLOCKBUSTER TRADE, SENDING FIVE PLAYERS TO VARI-OUS TEAMS TO BRING IN POINT GUARD TIM HARDAWAY AND FOUR OTHER PLAYERS. Because of the timing of the trade, the Heat's newly acquired players could not make the trip to Miami in time for a face-off against the world champion Bulls. "It was a throwaway game to me," Riley said. "We had eight guys. We had to hustle guard Tony Smith in here quick just to be legal." Although they were overmatched and outnumbered, the Heat came out of the locker room on fire. Heat guard Rex Chapman in par-ticular was in the zone, knocking down one three-pointer after another until the Heat had built a 26-point lead in the third quarter. When the Bulls made a late run, Chapman continued his hot shooting to preserve a 113–104 Miami victory. Chapman finished with a career-high 39 points, nailing 9 of his 10 three-point attempts. A stunned Coach Riley noted, "We still had … Rex, and Rex just had one of those nights."

HOSTILITY RAN HIGH AS THE HEAT SQUARED OFF AGAINST THE RIVAL KNICKS IN THE FIRST ROUND OF THE 1998 PLAYOFFS. In the 1997 postseason, the Heat had eliminated the Knicks in dramatic fashion by winning the last three games of the seven-game series, and the Knicks were ready to even the score. Emotions boiled over in Game 4 when Heat center Alonzo Mourning exchanged punches with his old Charlotte Hornets teammate, Knicks forward Larry Johnson. But tension turned to comedy when, in the middle of the fight, Mourning looked down and saw diminutive Knicks coach Jeff Van Gundy wrapped around his leg, eyes closed, holding on for dear life as he tried to break up the fight. "He was dangling on my leg," Mourning said. "It was like a piece of gum on my shoe." Both Mourning and Johnson drew suspensions for the fight. Van Gundy's punishment was seeing his picture in the newspapers the next day. The Knicks got the last laugh as they went on to win Game 5 and the series.

COURTSIDE STORIES

BIG FIGHT, LITTLE COACH

Alonzo Mourning tussles with Knicks forward Charles Oakley in 1997.

The Heat had high expectations going into their 10th-anniversary season. The team captured a second straight division title and met New York again in the first round of the playoffs. The Knicks came into the series still seething from the previous year's wrenching playoff defeat. The rematch was a tense affair, and tempers flared in Game 4 between Mourning and the Knicks' Johnson—former teammates in Charlotte. This time, in a reversal of fortune, it was the Heat who lost one of their best players to a suspension. Without Mourning, the Knicks won the deciding Game 5 in a 98–81 rout.

The 1998–99 season brought good news to Eastern Conference contenders such as the Heat. Michael Jordan had retired, and the Chicago Bulls' long stranglehold on the conference crown was finally over. At the end of a season shortened by a labor dispute between NBA players and owners, the Heat emerged with a 33–17 record and the top seed in the playoffs. Their first-round opponent was, once again, the Knicks. In the waning moments of the fifth and final game of the series, the Heat held a one-point lead, but New York had the ball. With a mere eight-tenths of a second on the clock, the Knicks' Houston threw up a running, one-handed shot that bounced high off the rim and then dropped in for a 78–77 New York win. The shot made the Knicks only the second eighth seed in the history of the NBA playoffs to defeat a number-one seed. "Life in basketball has a lot of suffering in it," Coach Riley said. "And we will suffer this one."

The Heat won a fourth consecutive division title in 1999–2000. Throughout the season, New York had nipped at Miami's heels for the division lead, and in round two of the playoffs, the archrivals faced off yet again. In another bruising series, the teams battled back and forth until

INTRODUCING...

PAT RILEY

COACH
HEAT SEASONS
1995–2003, 2005–08

PAT RILEY WAS AN NBA LEGEND BEFORE HE ARRIVED IN MIAMI, SO IT WAS OF LITTLE SURPRISE WHEN HE TURNED THE HEAT INTO AN EASTERN CONFERENCE POWERHOUSE. Riley arrived in South Florida in 1995 after a 4-year stint in New York, where he put together 4 seasons of 50-plus wins and led the Knicks to the 1994 NBA Finals. During his 1981 to 1990 tenure with the Los Angeles Lakers, Riley had averaged 59 wins a season at the helm of legendary "Showtime" Lakers teams that included NBA greats Kareem Abdul-Jabbar, Magic Johnson, and James Worthy. Already respected as a coach and evaluator of talent, Riley made a name for himself in Miami as a shrewd trader in the front office as well, bringing All-Stars Shaquille O'Neal, Alonzo Mourning, and Tim Hardaway to town. Riley's slicked-back hair and Armani suits gave him an image as precise and polished as his managing style. Former Lakers general manager Jerry West summed Riley up by saying, "He's inventive. He makes good, quick decisions. He has tremendous belief in himself and his role. He has the perfect temperament."

the final buzzer of Game 7. With barely two minutes remaining in that deciding game, Hardaway hit a three-pointer to give the Heat an 82–81 advantage. But on the next possession, New York's Ewing beat Mourning to the baseline for a dunk, and the Knicks held on for an 83–82 win— New York's third straight playoff series victory over the Heat.

Between 1997 and 2000, the Heat and the Knicks had met in the playoffs four consecutive times, and each year, the series had come down to the last possible game. Packed with fights and last-second wins, the rivalry stands as one of the most intense in NBA history. Coach Riley summed the rivalry up best by saying, "It might not have been the most artistic, but from an effort standpoint, from a defensive standpoint, from a competitive standpoint, where you are not going to give your man anything and he's not going to give you anything, it was some of the best basketball that's ever been played."

Guard Tim Hardaway dished out 1,947 career assists for the Heat, a feat that prompted the team to retire his jersey number (10) in 2009.

ALONZO MOURNING

WHEN PAT RILEY ARRIVED IN MIAMI, HE BELIEVED

THAT TO HAVE ANY CHANCE OF CONTENDING

FOR THE NBA CHAMPIONSHIP, THE HEAT WOULD

NEED A DOMINANT BIG MAN—AN INTIMIDATOR

IN THE PAINT AND A CENTER WITH A SOFT TOUCH

AROUND THE BUCKET. Riley got his man in 1995

when he traded for Alonzo Mourning. Mourning, known

to his teammates as "Zo," was a ferocious competitor.
He not only supplied the Heat with points, rebounds,
and blocked shots, but he was also the emotional
leader and competitive heart of the team, putting an ex-
clamation point on many of his biggest blocks and most
crucial points with a reverberating battle cry. Mourning
set the standard for work ethic in Miami, spending

hours in the weight room in the off-season. On March
30, 2009, the Heat retired Mourning's number 33
jersey. As the jersey was raised to the rafters before a
sold-out American Airlines Arena, Riley told Zo, "You
have sacrificed more than any other player we've ever
had in this franchise. And that's why we're raising these
numbers right here, forever."

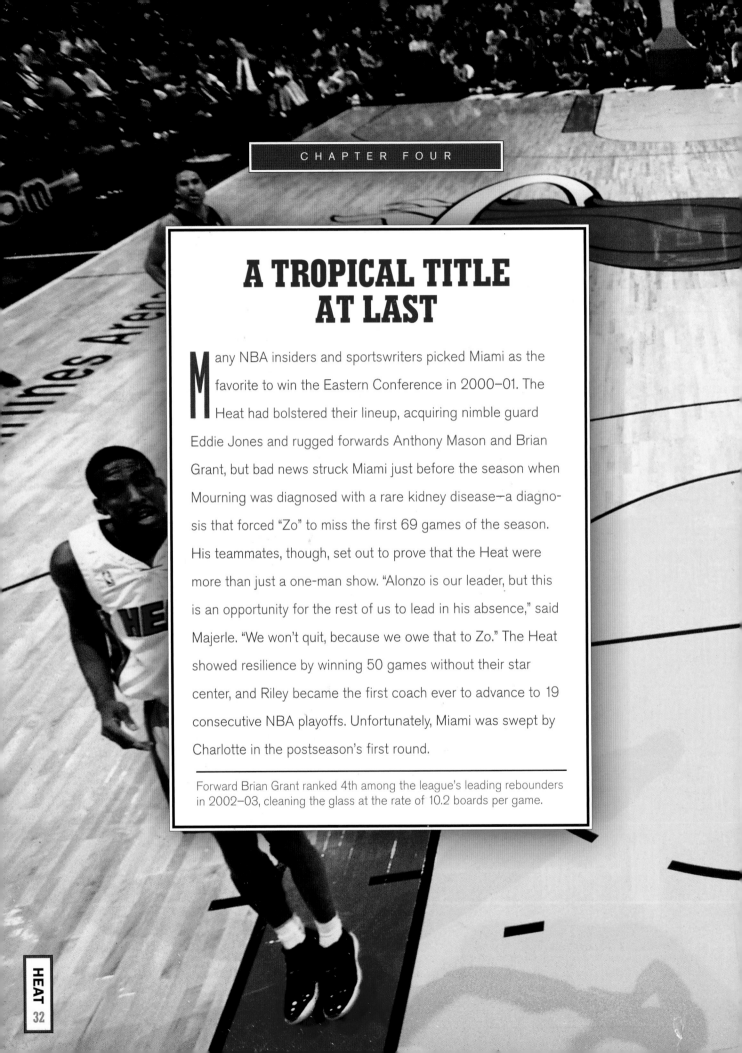

CHAPTER FOUR

A TROPICAL TITLE AT LAST

Many NBA insiders and sportswriters picked Miami as the favorite to win the Eastern Conference in 2000–01. The Heat had bolstered their lineup, acquiring nimble guard Eddie Jones and rugged forwards Anthony Mason and Brian Grant, but bad news struck Miami just before the season when Mourning was diagnosed with a rare kidney disease—a diagnosis that forced "Zo" to miss the first 69 games of the season. His teammates, though, set out to prove that the Heat were more than just a one-man show. "Alonzo is our leader, but this is an opportunity for the rest of us to lead in his absence," said Majerle. "We won't quit, because we owe that to Zo." The Heat showed resilience by winning 50 games without their star center, and Riley became the first coach ever to advance to 19 consecutive NBA playoffs. Unfortunately, Miami was swept by Charlotte in the postseason's first round.

Forward Brian Grant ranked 4th among the league's leading rebounders in 2002–03, cleaning the glass at the rate of 10.2 boards per game.

The next two seasons were among the bleakest in franchise history. Miami finished 2001–02 with a 36–46 record, and Riley's personal playoff streak ended. The 2002–03 campaign ended even worse, at 25–57, and Mourning left town. Although it seemed age had caught up with the Heat, Miami was already in rebuilding mode. In the 2002 NBA Draft, the club had selected swift forward Caron Butler. A year later, the Heat drafted highflying guard Dwyane Wade and signed multidimensional forward Lamar Odom as a free agent. Still, it would take another headline-making, Riley-engineered trade for the Heat to become an NBA powerhouse again.

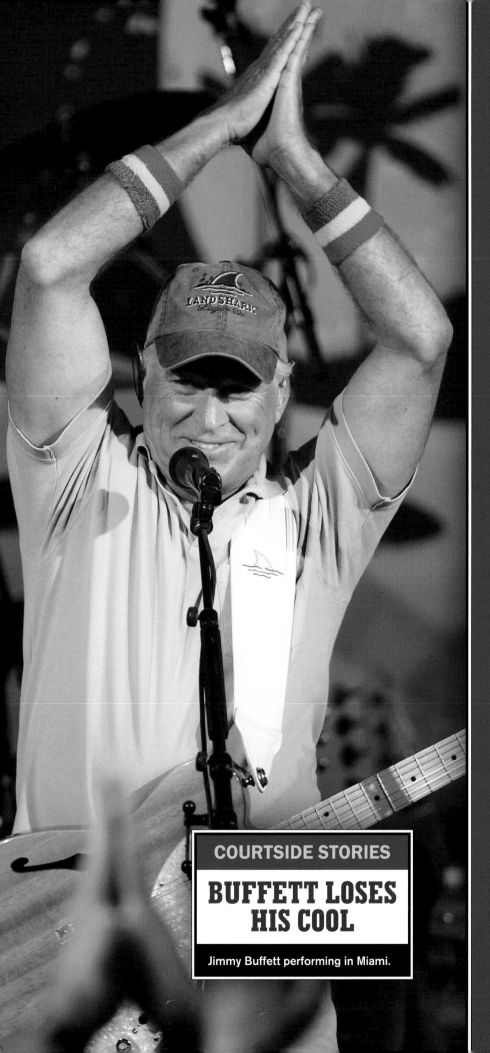

COURTSIDE STORIES

BUFFETT LOSES HIS COOL

Jimmy Buffett performing in Miami.

ON FEBRUARY 4, 2001, MUSICIAN AND AVID MIAMI HEAT FAN JIMMY BUFFETT—KNOWN FOR SUCH GOOD-TIME, LAID-BACK HITS AS "CHEESEBURGER IN PARADISE" AND "MARGARITAVILLE"—WAS ESCORTED FROM HIS COURTSIDE SEAT AT MIAMI'S AMERICAN AIRLINES ARENA. Miami and New York were locked in a tight game when Buffett let his passion get the better of him, loudly questioning the judgment of the referees. With about two minutes left in regulation, referee Joe Forte stopped the game and called security guards to escort Buffett from his seat. "There was a little boy sitting next to him, and a lady sitting by him," explained Forte. "He used some words he knows he shouldn't have used, so I asked security to move him to another location." Buffett watched his Heat finally fall to the Knicks in overtime, 103–100, from a tunnel in the arena. When asked if he had learned his lesson and planned to stop heckling referees, the Heat "superfan" said, "If my son's there, yes. If he's not, no. I was more afraid of going home and seeing my wife after the whole thing happened."

On July 14, 2004, Miami made just such a trade, acquiring All-Star center and three-time NBA Finals Most Valuable Player (MVP) Shaquille O'Neal from the Lakers. The Heat paid a heavy price by giving up Butler, Odom, Grant, and a first-round draft pick, but Riley was confident that O'Neal was the key to capturing a title. "Today," he said, "the Miami Heat took a giant step forward in our continued pursuit of an NBA championship for the city of Miami and this franchise."

After putting "Shaq" in Heat black and red, Miami brought back a familiar face in the middle of the 2004–05 season, reacquiring Alonzo Mourning from the New Jersey Nets to back up O'Neal. Wade, O'Neal, and Mourning powered the Heat to a 59–23 record and a playoff run to the 2005 Eastern Conference finals, where they faced the defending NBA champion Detroit Pistons. Although Wade played the series with a broken rib, and O'Neal was slowed by nagging injuries, Miami fought the Pistons tooth-and-nail all the way to the final minutes of an 88–82 loss in Game 7.

In the off-season, Riley added forwards Antoine Walker and James Posey and slick-passing point guard Jason Williams. With this retooled roster, Miami went 52–30 and made a return to the conference finals, where it again faced Detroit. Against the Pistons, Wade exploded to new heights of stardom. The vaunted Detroit defense had no answer for the

quickness of the guard known as "Flash," and the Heat won the series in six games to advance to their first NBA Finals.

Miami's prospects looked grim after the Heat lost the first two games of the 2006 Finals to star forward Dirk Nowitzki and the Dallas Mavericks. Miami was blown out by 14 points in Game 2, and all seemed lost in Game 3, with Miami down 13 points and only 6 minutes remaining on the clock. Then, however, Wade took over the game, engineering a comeback by calmly slicing through the Mavericks' defense and hitting one big shot after another. Behind the star guard, the Heat won Game 3 by a 98–96 score and never looked back, capturing the NBA title with four straight wins. Wade was named Finals MVP, and Riley finally delivered Miami the championship he had promised. "The great Pat Riley told me we were going to win today," O'Neal said after the game. "I didn't have the best game. But D-Wade's been doing it all year. He's the best player ever."

DWYANE WADE

DWYANE WADE GREW UP IN CHICAGO WATCHING MICHAEL JORDAN LEAD THE BULLS TO SIX NBA CHAMPIONSHIPS, AND AS SOON AS HE JOINED THE HEAT IN 2003, IT BECAME APPARENT HE HAD PICKED UP A FEW OF JORDAN'S MOVES ALONG THE WAY. Like Jordan, Wade possessed unreal athleticism and showcased a lightning-quick first step. Once he beat his man, he had the ability to either hit a short jumper, take the ball to the rim for the dunk, or dish to an open teammate. After Wade sliced through the tough Detroit defense early in the 2005 Eastern Conference finals, the Pistons began closing up the interior lanes in Game 4. Unable to penetrate to the basket, Wade struggled, and the Pistons dealt the Heat a painful defeat in the seven-game series. The following off-season, Dwyane spent hours in the gym improving his outside shot and learning to move without the ball so he wouldn't have to rely on his slashes to the hoop. The hard work paid off the next year, when the Heat won the 2006 NBA championship.

The first game of the 2006–07 season was a bad omen for the defending champs, who absorbed a 42-point drubbing at the hands of the Bulls. It didn't get much better after that. Wade and O'Neal went down with major injuries, and the Heat made the playoffs but were swept by Chicago in the first round.

The next season, the Heat cooled off further. Mourning blew out his right knee, and Miami never seemed to find its groove. Late in the season, Riley again made trade headlines, sending O'Neal to the Phoenix Suns for rangy forward Shawn Marion, officially ending the Heat's Wade–Shaq era. Just two seasons after winning the NBA championship, Miami finished with the league's worst record, 15–67.

DWYANE WADE COULDN'T WAIT TO DISTRIBUTE HOT-OFF-THE-PRESS COPIES OF *PEOPLE* MAGAZINE TO ALL OF HIS TEAMMATES ON APRIL 29, 2005. That's because Miami's star guard—best known for his explosive quickness and acrobatic shots—had been listed among the magazine's "50 Most Beautiful People" alongside Hollywood stars such as Julia Roberts, Brad Pitt, and Jennifer Aniston. "All of them will get a copy, no question," Wade said. His teammates were dreading the inevitable boasting. "We're going to be hearing about this for the rest of the year," guard Damon Jones said. The nomination started a tidal wave of recognition for Wade's off-court style. Shortly after appearing on the list, he was chosen to serve as ambassador for the fashionable Sean John clothing line. He was also named the NBA's best-dressed player for 2006 by *GQ* magazine and was cited by *Esquire* as one of the "Best Dressed Men in the World." Wade, however, wasn't the first Heat player to appear on *People*'s "50 Most Beautiful People" list—center Alonzo Mourning also made the cut in 1996.

Miami's only good fortune was that the horrible record gave the team the second overall pick in the 2008 NBA Draft, which it used to land high-scoring, 6-foot-9 forward Michael Beasley. Miami also made a draft-day trade to acquire rookie point guard Mario Chalmers, who had just led the University of Kansas Jayhawks to the 2008 national college championship. Miami fans witnessed a change in leadership as well, as Erik Spoelstra was named the club's new head coach, and Riley focused exclusively on his role as team president.

An outstanding athlete nicknamed "The Matrix," Shawn Marion averaged at least 13 points per game in each of his first 11 NBA seasons.

When the 2008–09 season kicked off, Wade made clear that his injury woes were behind him as he averaged an NBA-best 30.2 points per game. Beasley and Chalmers put forth quality rookie efforts, and after a late-season trade sent Marion to the Toronto Raptors for veteran center Jermaine O'Neal, the young Heat rose back above .500 and almost beat the Hawks in the first round of the playoffs. Miami's improvements were modest in 2009–10, as the Heat won 12 of their last 13 games but could not stay hot in the playoffs, suffering another first-round defeat, this time at the hands of the Boston Celtics.

Less than three months later, Miami fans found themselves on cloud nine. That's because in July 2010, the Heat landed the two most prized free agents in the NBA. The first to commit was former Toronto All-Star forward Chris Bosh. But Miami truly went into party mode when forward LeBron James, the former Cleveland Cavaliers superstar known as "King James," announced his intention to move south as well, giving Miami the most exciting trio in the league. "We are looking forward to the opportunity of building something that our fans in Miami will be proud of for a long, long time," said Riley. "The journey is just beginning."

INTRODUCING...

MICHAEL BEASLEY

POSITION FORWARD
HEIGHT 6-FOOT-9
HEAT SEASONS 2008–10

THERE WERE NOT MANY BASKET-BALL INSIDERS WHO DOUBTED MICHAEL BEASLEY'S POTENTIAL, BUT NO ONE THOUGHT HE HAD A CHANCE OF WINNING THE NBA MVP AWARD AT THE END OF HIS ROOKIE SEASON. No one, that is, except Michael Beasley. "I don't ever want to be second best," the rookie said after a Heat preseason practice in 2008. "I feel I can walk down those steps to the locker room and be better than everybody else. I think going for Rookie of the Year is selling myself short." During his single season at Kansas State University, Beasley certainly had backed up his braggadocio, averaging 26.2 points and 12.4 boards per game to earn All-American honors. Beasley's size, athleticism, and confidence translated into a promising rookie season as a pro, as he netted 13.9 points per game. Although he didn't win the MVP or any other major awards, he was in good hands—former Heat star Alonzo Mourning, a regular at Miami practices, was watching him. "I'm going to stay on him, because I see nothing but the best in him." In 2010, Beasley was traded away as Miami shook up its roster.

The Miami Heat have been increasing the already hot temperature in southern Florida for more than 20 years. While the franchise might be one of the youngest in the NBA, it has treated basketball fans in Miami to some of the greatest playoff games in NBA history, the leadership of a legendary coach, and the play of two future Hall of Fame centers. With today's new-look Heat rising toward championship heights once more, Miami may soon be the center of the hoops world again.

Mixing youngsters such as Mario Chalmers (below) and veterans such as Jermaine O'Neal (opposite), Miami made a run to the 2010 playoffs.

INDEX